FUN JOKES!

FOR FUNNY KIDS

Reader's
Digest

New York / Montreal

A Note from the Editors

Reader's Digest is the world's #1 collector of humor—for everyone from age 6 to 106. In *Fun Jokes for Funny Kids*, we've compiled the best of the best for our youngest readers. We asked one witty girl to tell us which ones she liked most; you'll see Alexa's Favorites sprinkled throughout the book.

Now we're inviting parents of budding comedians to send jokes for our next volume. Submit your child's riddles, one-liners, puns, and more at **rd.com/jokesforkids**.

About Alexa

Alexa is a second-grader who lives in New York City. She loves gymnastics, tacos, and the color pink.

Table of Contents

Knock!
Knock!

Who's there...?

Alpaca

Knock! Knock!
  Who's there?
Alpaca.
  Alpaca who?
Alpaca the suitcase, you load up the car!

Howlin' for You

Knock! Knock!
  Who's there?
Howl.
  Howl who?
Howl you know if you don't open the door?

Beets

Knock! Knock!
  Who's there?
Beets.
  Beets who?
Beets me!

Two Knee

Knock! Knock!
   Who's there?
Two knee.
   Two knee who?
Two knee fish!

- - - - - - - - - - ★ **ALEXA'S FAVORITE**

Abe Who?

Knock! Knock!
   Who's there?
Abe.
   Abe who?
Abe...CDEFGH

- -

Ketchup

Knock! Knock!
   Who's there?
Ketchup.
   Ketchup who?
Ketchup with me and I'll tell you!

Cargo Who?

Knock, Knock
  Who's there?
Cargo!
  Cargo who?
Car go beep, beep!

Kanga

Knock! Knock!
  Who's there?
Kanga.
  Kanga who?
Actually, it's kangaroo.

Closure

Knock! Knock!
  Who's there?
Closure.
  Closure who?
Closure mouth while you're chewing!

Déja

Knock! Knock!
  Who's there?
Déja.
  Déja who?
Knock! Knock!

Dishes

Knock! Knock!
  Who's there?
Dishes.
  Dishes who?
Dishes a nice place you got here.

Art

Knock! Knock!
  Who's there?
Art.
  Art who?
R2-D2, of course.

--------- ★ **ALEXA'S FAVORITE**

Ben

Knock! Knock!
   Who's there?
Ben.
   Ben who?
Ben knocking for 20 minutes!

Sherlock

Knock! Knock!
   Who's there?
Sherlock.
   Sherlock who?
Sherlock your door.

Owls Say

Knock! Knock!
   Who's there?
Owls say.
   Owls say who?
Yes, they do.

Olive

Knock! Knock!
   Who's there?
Olive.
   Olive who?
Olive you and I don't care who knows it!

Loaf

Knock! Knock!
   Who's there?
Loaf.
   Loaf who?
I don't just like bread, I loaf it.

Extraterrestrial

Knock! Knock!
   Who's there?
An extraterrestrial.
   An extraterrestrial who?
Wait—how many extraterrestrials do you know?

Turnip

Knock! Knock!
Who's there?
Turnip.
Turnip who?
Turnip the volume. I love this song!

Figs

Knock! Knock!
Who's there?
Figs.
Figs who?
Figs your doorbell. it's not working!

Alex

Knock! Knock!
Who's there?
Alex.
Alex who?
Hey, Alex the questions around here!

Funny Nun

Knock, knock
   Who's there?
Nun.
   Nun who?
Nun of your business!

Isabelle

Knock! Knock!
   Who's there?
Isabelle.
   Isabelle who?
Isabelle working, or should I keep knocking?

Eyesore Who?

Knock! Knock!
   Who's there?
Eyesore.
   Eyesore who?
Eyesore do love you!

Honeybee

Knock! Knock!
Who's there?
Honeybee.
Honeybee who?
Honeybee a dear and open the door, please.

No One

Knock! Knock!
Who's there?
No one.
No one who?
Silence

Ice Cream

Knock! Knock!
Who's there?
Ice cream.
Ice cream who?
Ice cream right now if you DON'T LET ME IN!

---------- ★ **ALEXA'S FAVORITE**

Canoe

Knock! Knock!
   Who's there?
Canoe.
   Canoe who?
Canoe open the door?

- -

Leaf Who?

Knock! Knock!
   Who's there?
Leaf.
   Leaf Who?
Leaf me alone!

Boo Who?

Knock! Knock!
   Who's there?
Boo.
   Boo who?
It's me. Why are you crying?

Goat

Knock! Knock!

Who's there?

Goat.

Goat who?

Goat to the door to see who's knocking!

Cow Who?

Knock! Knock!

Who's there?

Cow.

Cow who?

Cows don't "who," they "MOO."

Little Old Lady

Knock! Knock!

Who's there?

A little old lady.

A little old lady who?

I didn't know you could yodel!

Control Freak

Knock! Knock!

Who's there?

Control Freak.

Con—

Okay, now you say, "Control freak who?"

Spell

Knock! Knock!

Who's there?

Spell.

Spell who?

W-H-O

Nana

Knock! Knock!

Who's there?

Nana.

Nana who?

Nana your business who's there.

Noah

Knock! Knock!
   Who's there?
Noah.
   Noah who?
Noah any place I can get a bite to eat?

- - - - - - - - - - ★ **ALEXA'S FAVORITE**

Annie

Knock! Knock!
   Who's there?
Annie.
   Annie who?
Annie body going to open the door already?

- -

Orange

Knock! Knock!
   Who's there?
Orange.
   Orange who?
Orange you gonna open the door?

Wire Who?

Knock! Knock!
  Who's there?
Wire.
  Wire who?
Wire you always asking, 'Who's there'?

Scold

Knock! Knock!
  Who's there?
Scold.
  Scold who?
Scold outside—let me in!

Lettuce

Knock! Knock!
  Who's there?
Lettuce.
  Lettuce who?
Lettuce in already!

Police

Knock! Knock!
Who's there?
Police.
Police who?
Police hurry—I'm freezing out here!

Otto

Knock! Knock!
Who's there?
Otto.
Otto who?
Otto know what's taking you so long!

Doris

Knock! Knock!
Who's there?
Doris.
Doris who?
Doris locked. Open up!

Radio Who?

Knock! Knock!
Who's there?
Radio.
Radio who?
Radio not, here I come!

Amos

Knock! Knock!
Who's there?
Amos.
Amos who?
A mosquito bit me!

Luke

Knock! Knock!
Who's there?
Luke.
Luke who?
Luke through the keyhole to see!

Ho-Ho Who?

Knock! Knock!

Who's there?

Ho-ho.

Ho-ho who?

You know, your Santa impression could use a little work.

Impatient Cow

Knock! Knock!

Who's there?

Impatient cow.

Impatient co—

MOO!

Stopwatch

Knock! Knock!

Who's there?

Stopwatch.

Stopwatch who?

Stopwatch you're doing and pay attention!

Tank

Knock! Knock!
  Who's there?
Tank.
  Tank who?
You're welcome!

---------- ★ **ALEXA'S FAVORITE**

Cash

Knock! Knock!
  Who's there?
Cash.
  Cash who?
No thanks, but I'd love some peanuts!

Doorbell

Knock! Knock!
  Who's there?
Somebody who can't reach the doorbell!

Ridiculous
Riddles

Oh, "AI" get it!

Q: I am a word that begins with the letter I. If you add the letter A to me, I become a new word with a different meaning which sounds exactly the same. What word am I?

A: Isle (add A to make "Aisle")

Count the Days

Q: Can you name three consecutive days without using the words "Wednesday," "Friday," or "Sunday"?

A: Yesterday, today, and tomorrow.

Yellow I Look...

Q: Yellow I look and massive I weigh. In the morning I come to brighten your day. What am I?

A: A school bus.

You Can Keep It

Q: You can break me without touching me or even seeing me. What am I?

A: A promise.

What Do You Throw Out...

Q: What do you throw out when you want to use it, but take in when you don't want to use it?

A: An anchor.

---------- ★ ALEXA'S FAVORITE

Very Confusing

Q: What comes once in a minute, twice in a moment, but never in a thousand years?

A: The letter "m."

- -

Odd, Indeed

Q: I'm an odd number. If you take away one of the letters in my name, I become even. What number am I?

A: Seven. (Take away the S!)

Echo

Q: Many have heard me, but no one has seen me, and I will not speak back until spoken to. What am I?

A: An echo!

All Ears

Q: What has hundreds of ears but can't hear a thing?

A: A cornfield!

A Tall Tale

Q: A girl fell off of a 30-foot ladder, but she didn't get hurt at all. How is this possible?

A: She fell off the bottom step!

Cat in a Box

Q: How many cats can you put in an empty box?

A: One. After that, the box isn't empty anymore.

I am the Beginning...

Q: I am the beginning of the end, and the end of time and space. I am essential to creation, and I surround every place. Who am I?

A: The letter E!

I Travel All Over...

Q: I travel all over the world but always stay in my corner. What am I?

A: A stamp!

--------- ★ **ALEXA'S FAVORITE**

What Do You Break...

Q: What do you break before you use it?

A: An egg!

A Man Is Pushing His Car...

Q: A man is pushing his car along, and when he comes to a hotel, he shouts, "I'm bankrupt!" Why?

A: He's playing Monopoly.

Land and T

Q: Why is an island like the letter T?

A: They're both in the middle of water!

Just Like Magic

Q: A magician promises that he can throw a ball as hard as he can and have it stop, change direction, and come back to him. He claims he can do it without the ball bouncing off of anything, the ball being tied to anything, or the use of magnets. How is this possible?

A: He throws the ball straight up in the air!

A Word I Know...

Q: This word I know? Six letters it contains. Take away the last ... and only twelve remains. What is the word?

A: "Dozens"

I Have a Head But No Body...

Q: I have a head but no body, a heart but no blood. Just leaves and no branches, I grow without wood. What am I?

A: Lettuce!

Magic Number

Q: How do you make the number one disappear?

A: Add the letter G and then presto— it's Gone!

A Seal-y Riddle

Q: What starts with "e," ends with "e," and contains one letter?

A: An envelope!

What Only Gets Wetter...

Q: What only gets wetter the more it dries?

A: A towel!

Nose or Foot?

Q: Why can't your nose be 12 inches long?

A: Because then it'd be a foot.

Which Month Has...

Q: Which month has 28 days?

A: All of them, silly!

Take a Second Look

Q: How many seconds are there in a year?

A: Twelve—January 2nd, February 2nd, March 2nd...

A Red House...

Q: If a red house is made of red bricks, has a red wooden door, and a red roof, and a yellow house is made of yellow bricks, has a yellow wooden door, and a yellow roof, then what is a green house made of?

A: Glass.

What Can Run But Never Walks...

Q: What can run but never walks? Has a mouth but never talks? Has a head but never weeps? Has a bed but never sleeps?

A: A river.

Capping It Off

Q: I have a neck but no head, and I wear a cap. What am I?

A: A bottle!

---------- ★ **ALEXA'S FAVORITE**

More Is Less

Q: What five-letter word becomes shorter if you add two letters to it?

A: "Short" (add "er")!

Wooden Case

Q: I am taken from a mine and shut up in a wooden case, from which I am never released, and yet I am used by almost everybody.

A: Pencil lead.

The Elephant in the Room

Q: I'm the size of an elephant, but I weigh nothing. What am I?

A: An elephant's shadow!

Shhhh....

Q: What is so delicate that saying its name breaks it?

A: Silence.

What Do You Call...

Q: What do you call a parade of rabbits hopping backward?

A: A receding hare-line.

What Is Easy to Get Into...

Q: What is easy to get into but hard to get out of?

A: Trouble.

Red Bite, Green Bite

Q: When do you go at red and stop at green?

A: When you're eating a watermelon.

Apple Tree

Q: How many apples grow on a tree?

A: All of them.

Numbers

Q: If two's company, and three's a crowd, what are 4 and 5?

A: 9!

What Did Zero Say...

Q: What did zero say to eight?

A: Nice belt.

A Rock-Solid Joke

Q: What rock group consists of four famous men but none of them sing?

A: The faces on Mount Rushmore!

Beary Tricky

Q: There is a house with four walls. All of the walls are facing south. A bear is circling the house. What color is the bear?

A: White. If all walls of the house are facing south, the house must be on the North Pole, so the bear is a polar bear.

- - - - - - - - - ★ **ALEXA'S FAVORITE**

What Starts with a P...

Q: What starts with a P, ends with an E, and has thousands of letters?

A: The post office!

- -

Where Is the Ocean...

Q: Where is the ocean the deepest?

A: On the bottom!

How Many Bananas...

Q: How many bananas can you eat if your stomach is empty?

A: Just one—after that, it's not empty anymore.

Why is the Letter A...

Q: Why is the letter A the most like a flower?

A: Because the B is after it.

Tell This One Out Loud!

Q: One (k)night a king and a queen went into a castle. There was no one in the castle when they went in, and no one else entered the castle while they were there. The next day, three people came out of the castle. Who were they?

A: The king, the queen, and the knight!

What's in a name?

Q: What belongs to you but is used more by others?

A: Your name.

Apples 2 Apples

Q: There are three apples on a table and you take away two of them. How many apples do you have now?

A: Two, of course!

...Unless You Want To Be Wrong, Of Course

Q: What question can you never answer "yes" to?

A: What does N-O spell?

You Might Have To Sleep on This One

Q: What has one head, one foot, and four legs?

A: A bed.

The Deadly Rooms

Q: A prisoner is forced to go into one of three rooms, but he can choose which room. The first room is ablaze with fire. The second one is rigged with explosives that will go off as soon as he enters. The third contains a pair of lions who haven't eaten in years. Which room should he choose to survive?

A: The third room—any lions who hadn't eaten in years would be dead!

What Kind of Cheese...

Q: What kind of cheese is made backward?

A: Edam.

One-Liners

Always Silent

• • •

If you arrest a mime, do you still have to tell him he has the right to remain silent?

Bothersome Questions

• • •

Don't you hate it when someone answers their own questions? I do.

Can't Hide

• • •

I keep trying to lose weight, but it keeps finding me.

Made You Laugh

• • •

Skeletons are great at stand-up comedy—when they use their funny bone.

Moon Dining

• • •

Did you hear about the restaurant on the moon? Great food, no atmosphere.

Customer Service

• • •

If the customer is always right, then why isn't everything free?

The Fur Is Flying

• • •

Cat to Owner: Why are you so upset that I shed on the couch—it's called fur-niture!

- - - - - - - - - ★ ALEXA'S FAVORITE

Doing Time

• • •

Did you hear about the crook who stole a calendar—he got twelve months.

Early Morning Revelations

• • •

I woke up this morning and forgot
which side the sun rises from;
then it dawned on me.

Underwater

• • •

What do fish say when they hit a
concrete wall?...Dam!

Late-Night Munchies

• • •

If we shouldn't eat at night, why do
they put a light in the fridge?

Tough Sentencing

• • •

Did you hear about the semicolon
that broke the law?
He was given two consecutive sentences.

A Little Levity

• • •

I'm reading a great book about antigravity—
I just can't put it down.

Ode to Tortillas

• • •

I've just written a song about tortillas;
actually, it's more of a rap.

Rolling with Laughter

• • •

Did you hear the one about the little
mountain? It's Hill-arious!

No Onion, No Cry

• • •

A lot of people cry when they cut onions.
The trick is not to form an
emotional bond.

Time Weighs On

• • •

Did you hear about the hungry clock?
He went back four seconds.

- - - - - - - - - ★ **ALEXA'S FAVORITE**

Cannibal Humor

• • •

Two cannibals are eating a clown.
One cannibal turns to the other and asks,
"This taste funny to you?"

- -

Contradiction

• • •

Seen on the door of a repair shop:
WE CAN FIX ANYTHING. (Please knock on
the door—the bell doesn't work.)

The Joy of Discovery

• • •

I think the Discovery Channel should be
on a different channel every day.

Oil Origins

• • •

If corn oil comes from corn, where does
baby oil come from?

Coming Through!

• • •

Two fish are in a tank. One says to the other,
"Do you know how to drive this thing?"

When a Dolphin Makes
a Mistake...

• • •

Did you hear about the dolphin
who kept messing up?
He doesn't do it on porpoise.

Rainy Day

• • •

Plan ahead. It wasn't raining when
Noah built the ark.

When an Otter Needs
Personal Space

• • •

Get otter here!

Star Trek Cat

• • •

Live long and pawspurr.

Feeling Pretty Proud
of Myself

• • •

The Sesame Street puzzle I bought said
3-5 years, but I finished it in 18 months.

Velcro

• • •

Velcro—what a rip-off!

Car Wash

• • •

A dad is washing the car with his son.
After a moment the son asks his father,
"Do you think we could use a
sponge instead?"

Screensaver Question

• • •

I often wonder about people who live
in tropical destinations. What do their
screensavers look like?

The Right to Remain Silent

• • •

The world tongue-twister champion just got
arrested. I hear they're gonna give him a
really tough sentence.

Wacky
Animals

Anxious Dino

Q: What do you call anxious dinosaurs?

A: Nervous Rex.

---------- ★ **ALEXA'S FAVORITE**

Elephant Vacation

Q: What did the baby elephant ask his mom before they left for vacation?

A: "Can I borrow a suitcase? I only have a little trunk."

Cat Computer

Q: Why was the cat sitting on the computer?

A: He was keeping an eye on the mouse!

Bear Caught in the Rain

Q: What do you call a wet bear?

A: A drizzly bear.

Duck Feathers

Q: Which side of a duck has the most feathers?

A: The outside.

Frozen Accounts

Q: Where do polar bears keep their money?

A: In a snowbank!

A Pork Sport

Q: Why shouldn't you play basketball with a pig?

A: Because it'll hog the ball!

Scottish Terrier

Q: How did the little Scottish dog feel when he saw a monster?

A: Terrier-fied!

I've Had It—Up to My Neck

Q: What did the giraffe say when her neighbor wouldn't stop talking?

A: You're giraffing me crazy.

Charging Bull

Q: What's the first thing you should do if a bull charges you?

A: Pay him!

Can You Mooooove?

Q: What do you get from a pampered cow?

A: Spoiled milk.

Scaredy Cat

Q: Why did the cat run away from the tree?

A: It was scared of its bark.

---------- ★ **ALEXA'S FAVORITE**

Confused Dolphin

Q: What does a dolphin say when he's confused?

A: Can you please be more Pacific?

Bear Ears

Q: What would bears be without bees?

A: Ears

Why Aren't Dogs...

Q: Why aren't dogs good dancers?

A: Because they have two left feet!

Igloo House

Q: How does a penguin build its house?

A: Igloos it together.

Toad Parking

Q: What did the toad say when he parked illegally?

A: "Just waiting for the bus because my car got toad."

Emotional Farm Animals

Q: What do you get if you cross an angry sheep and a moody cow?

A: An animal that's in a baaaaaaaaad moooooooooooood.

---------- ★ **ALEXA'S FAVORITE**

Bees in the Rain

Q: Can bees fly in the rain?

A: Not without their yellow jackets.

Fishy Fitness

Q: Why are fish so good at watching their weight?

A: Because they have lots of scales!

Bones in Trees?

Q: Why do dogs bury bones in the ground?

A: Because they can't bury them in trees!

Shorthaired Cat

Q: What do you call a kitten that cuts her hair really short?

A: A bob cat!

Animal Care

Q: What do you call a cat that joins the Red Cross?

A: A first-aid kit.

Get a Buzz Cut?

Q: Why is a bee's hair always sticky?

A: Because it uses a honey comb!

Chocolate

Q: What's a cat's favorite dessert?

A: Chocolate mousse.

Hello to You Too

Q: What is every whale's favorite greeting?

A: Whale hello there!

Relationship Issues

Q: What did the wild cat couple yell during their argument?

A: "You're such a cheetah!"
"No, you're lion!"

Hope You're Not Lactose Intolerant

Q: If you have 15 cows and 5 goats, what would you have?

A: Plenty of milk!

A Little Bird Whispered...

Q: What do you call two birds in love?

A: Tweet-hearts!

Leopard Lunch

Q: What did the leopard say after finishing a delicious meal?

A: "That hit the spot!"

Awkward Encounters

Q: What did the bird-watcher say when she mistook a hawk for an eagle?

A: Well, this is hawkward.

Prickly Pet

Q: What do you get when you cross a turtle with a porcupine?

A: A slowpoke.

Over-Caffeinated Kangaroo

Q: Why did the kangaroo stop drinking coffee?

A: She got too jumpy!

Swimming Preferences

Q: Why do seals swim in salt water?

A: Because pepper water makes them sneeze.

The Hardest-Working Chicken You'll Ever Meet

Q: How long do chickens work?

A: Around the cluck!

---------- ★ **ALEXA'S FAVORITE**

Beautiful Music

Q: Where do orcas hear music?

A: Orca-stras!

Vacay, Baby!

Q: Where did the sheep go on vacation?

A: The baaaahamas.

Tornado Cow

Q: Whatever happened to the cow that was lifted into the air by the tornado?

A: Udder disaster!

Baby Monkey

Q: What do you call a baby monkey?

A: A chimp off the old block.

---------- ★ **ALEXA'S FAVORITE**

Astro Fish

Q: Where are fish in orbit?

A: In trout-er space.

Ommm

Q: What do you call a large dog that meditates?

A: Aware wolf.

Hummingbirds

Q: Why do hummingbirds hum?

A: Because they can't remember the words.

Whatta Ham

Q: What do you get when you play tug-of-war with a pig?

A: Pulled pork.

Cat Fight

Q: What do cats do after having an argument?

A: Hiss and make up.

The Big Apple

Q: Why do cows go to New York?

A: To see the moosicals!

Lazy Birds

Q: Why do birds fly south in the fall?

A: Because it's too far to walk.

Elephant for Hire

Q: Why didn't the elephant get the job he wanted?

A: His qualifications were completely irrelephant.

Quirky
Q&A's

You Butter Be Quiet

Q: Did you hear the one about the greedy peanut butter?

A: I'm not telling you. You might spread it.

Teddy Bears

Q: Why are teddy bears never hungry?

A: Because they're always stuffed.

Never Trust a Veggie

Q: Why shouldn't you tell a secret on a farm?

A: Because the potatoes have eyes and the corn has ears.

Burger Dance

Q: Where do beef burgers go to dance?

A: The meatball.

Umbrellas Up

Q: What goes up when the rain comes down?

A: An umbrella.

---------- ★ ALEXA'S FAVORITE

Peter Pan

Q: Why is Peter Pan always flying?

A: Because he never lands.

Ships, Ahoy!

Q: What happened to the pirate ship that sank in the sea full of sharks?

A: It came back with a skeleton crew!

Car Jack

Q: How do you lift a frozen car?

A: With a Jack Frost.

- - - - - - - - - ★ **ALEXA'S FAVORITE**

Jungle Poker

Q: Why don't cats play poker in the jungle?

A: There are too many cheetahs.

- -

Escar-Don't-Go

Q: Why do French people eat snails?

A: Because they won't touch fast food.

Healthy As a Horse

Q: Why are most horses in shape?

A: Because they are on a stable diet.

Good Night Gingy

Q: What does the gingerbread man use to make his bed?

A: Cookie sheets!

Fisherman Magic

Q: What did the fisherman say to the magician?

A: Pick a cod, any cod.

Hidden Talents

Q: Why did the invisible man turn down the job offer?

A: Because he just couldn't see himself doing it.

Turn That Frown Upside Down

Q: What do you call cheese that is sad?

A: Blue cheese.

Roof Shingles

Q: What did the hail storm say to the roof?

A: Hang on to your shingles; this will be no ordinary sprinkles.

Runaway Bagel

Q: How do you keep a bagel from getting away?

A: Put lox on it.

How Cats Drive

Q: What kind of sports car does a cat drive?

A: A Furrari.

Golden Retriever

Q: What do you get if you cross a gold dog with a telephone?

A: A golden retriever.

How Many Sheep...

Q: How many sheep does it take to make one sweater?

A: Depends how well they can knit.

Lazy Weather

Q: What type of cloud is so lazy, because it will never get up?

A: Fog!

On the Scene

Q: Did you hear about the carrot detective?

A: He got to the root of every case.

---------- ★ **ALEXA'S FAVORITE**

Lost Balloons Never Bothered Her Anyway

Q: Why shouldn't you give Elsa a balloon?

A: Because she'll let it go!

Snow Kids

Q: What do snowmen call their offspring?

A: Chill-dren.

Raindrop Convo

Q: What did one raindrop say to the other?

A: Two's company, three's a cloud.

Mickey's Career Change

Q: Why did Mickey Mouse become an astronaut?

A: So he could visit Pluto!

Not Your Cheese

Q: What do you call cheese that isn't yours?

A: Nacho cheese.

She Shoots, She Scores!

Q: Why should you never break up with a goalie?

A: Because he's a keeper.

Likely Not Far

Q: Where do you find a no-legged dog?

A: Right where you left him.

Homework

Q: Why did the student eat his homework?

A: Because the teacher told him it was a piece of cake!

Shoe Sleeper

Q: What do you call a cat sleeping in your shoe?

A: A puss in boots.

Queen's Rain

Q: What is a queen's favorite kind of precipitation?

A: Reign!

The Sick Giant

Q: Did you hear about the giant who threw up?

A: It's all over town.

Eye of the Hurricane

Q: How does a hurricane see?

A: With its eye.

---------- ★ **ALEXA'S FAVORITE**

Education Got You Down?

Q: Why was the math book sad?

A: Because it had so many problems.

- -

Comb ON!

Q: What did the bald man exclaim when he received a comb for a present?

A: Gee, I'll never part with it!

The Snowman's Baby

Q: What did the snowman and his wife put over their baby's crib?

A: A snowmobile!

How Distasteful

Q: What happened when the cannibal arrived late to the dinner party?

A: He received the cold shoulder.

Rock On!

Q: What do you call blueberries playing the guitar?

A: A jam session.

The Glass Slippers Don't Help...

Q: Why is Cinderella so bad at soccer?

A: Because she always runs away from the ball!

Country of Nauru

Q: Do you know the country of Nauru has no capital?

A: That's why it starts with a lowercase letter.

Space Computer

Q: What's an astronaut's favorite part of a computer?

A: The space bar.

Toilet Talk

Q: What did one toilet say to the other toilet?

A: You look flushed.

Mail

Q: What letters are not in the alphabet?

A: The ones in the mail.

---------- ★ **ALEXA'S FAVORITE**

An Unbalanced Bike

Q: Why do bicycles fall over?

A: Because they are two-tired.

Rain Feast

Q: Why did the man use ketchup in the rain?

A: Because it was raining cats and hot dogs.

Watermelon

Q: Why did the melon jump into the lake?

A: He wanted to be a watermelon.

Sick

Q: What do you give a lemon that's sick.

A: Lemon-aid.

Trusty Dog

Q: **What do you get when you cross a dog and a calculator?**

A: A friend you can count on.

---------- ★ **ALEXA'S FAVORITE**

A Stroke of Genius

Q: **Why did the golfer wear two pairs of pants?**

A: In case he got a hole in one.

Eye to Eye

Q: **What did the left eye say to the right eye?**

A: Between us, something smells!

Cold Nut

Q: **What did the nut say when it got a cold?**

A: Cashew.

Duck

Q: What time is it when people are throwing pieces of bread at your head?

A: Time to duck.

Weather Money

Q: Why did the woman go outdoors with her purse open?

A: Because she expected some change in the weather.

High School

Q: Why did the boy bring the ladder to school?

A: Because he was going to high school.

It's a Ruff Job

Q: How do dog catchers get paid?

A: By the pound!

Moon

Q: How do you know when the moon has had enough to eat?

A: When it's full.

A Snowman's Lunch

Q: What do snowmen eat for lunch?

A: Icebergers.

Shake It Up

Q: What do you get when you cross a cow with a trampoline?

A: A milkshake.

Dangerous Precipitation

Q: What do you call dangerous precipitation?

A: A rain of terror.

Cats Aren't Winners

Q: What is it called when a cat wins a dog show?

A: A CAT-HAS-TROPHY!

Policeman Joke

Q: What did the policeman say to his belly button?

A: You're under a vest.

Lightning Love

Q: What did the lightning bolt say to the other lightning bolt?

A: You're shocking!

Very Slippery

Q: What's a banana peel's favorite type of shoe?

A: Slippers!

Perfect
Puns

Baseball Nut

• • •

Ray's friends claim he's a baseball nut.
He says they're way off base.

Cloudy with a Chance
of Reindeer

• • •

Mrs. Claus looked up at the sky and said to
Santa, "Looks like rain, dear!"

String Fight

• • •

My older sister used to hit me with
stringed instruments—if only I had known
about her history of violins.

Antenna Love

• • •

Two antennas met on a roof, fell in love, and
got married. The ceremony wasn't much,
but the reception was excellent.

Mark It Up
• • •

I'm a big fan of whiteboards.
I find them quite re-markable.

Toucans
• • •

A friend of mine tried to annoy me
with bird puns, but I soon realized that
toucan play at that game.

Way with Words
• • •

Don't interrupt someone working
intently on a puzzle.
Chances are, you'll hear some crosswords.

---------- ★ ALEXA'S FAVORITE

Chilly Chilly
• • •

What do you call a cold dog? A chilli dog.

- -

Either Oar

• • •

The boating store was having a big sale on canoes. It was quite an oar deal.

Cheesy

• • •

Did you hear about the cheese factory that exploded in France?
There was nothing left but de Brie.

Pricey Candy

• • •

The price of candy at the movie theater is ridiculous. They're always raisinet!

Time on My Side

• • •

I was going to make myself a belt made out of watches, but then I realized it would be a waist of time.

Clown Courtesy

• • •

Yesterday a clown held the door open for me. It was such a nice jester!

Brain Transplant

• • •

I wasn't originally going to get a brain transplant, but then I changed my mind.

Baking Pig

• • •

Did you hear my pig got hired by the local restaurant? He was really good at bacon.

Funny Hot Dog

• • •

Did you see the movie about the hot dog? It was an Oscar Wiener.

Octopus or Cat?

• • •

My cat has eight legs and likes to swim.
He's an octo-puss.

- -

Silk Ties

• • •

Did you hear about the two silkworms
in a race? It ended in a tie!

RIP

• • •

Did you hear about the man who was
accidentally buried alive?
It was a grave mistake.

Break a Leg

• • •

Why do we tell actors to "break a leg?"
Because every play has a cast.

Zen and the Art of Breakfast

• • •

Hear about the new restaurant called Karma? There's no menu—you get what you deserve.

Lost Luggage

• • •

I tried to sue the airport for misplacing my luggage—I lost my case.

Soda to the Head

• • •

Did you hear about the guy who got hit in the head with a can of soda?
He was lucky it was a soft drink.

Funny Fowl

• • •

My duck that loves making jokes?
He's a real wise-quacker!

Hilarious
Holidays

Valentine's Day

Beating Hearts

Q: What did one beet say to the other on Valentine's Day?

A: You make my heart beet faster!

Pointy Love

Q: Did you hear about the nearsighted porcupine?

A: He fell in love with a pin cushion!

Buzz-Buzz

Q: What did the boy bee say to the girl bee on Valentine's Day?

A: You are bee-utiful!

---------- ★ **ALEXA'S FAVORITE**

Dating Bats

Q: What did the bat say to his girlfriend?

A: You're fun to hang around with.

- -

Squirrel Gifts

Q: What do squirrels give for Valentine's Day?

A: Forget-me-nuts.

Flower Mistake

Q: What kind of flowers do you never give on Valentine's Day?

A: Cauliflowers!

Volcano Romance

Q: What did one volcano say to the other?

A: I lava you.

Sweets for the Sweet

Q: Why shouldn't you fall in love with a pastry chef?

A: He'll dessert you.

---------- ★ **ALEXA'S FAVORITE**

Hop-Hop Love

Q: What did the rabbit say to his girlfriend on Valentine's Day?

A: Somebunny loves you!

I'll Call You

Q: How did the phone propose to his girlfriend on Valentine's Day?

A: He gave her a ring.

Love Stinks

Q: Why do skunks love Valentine's Day?

A: Because they're scent-imental creatures!

Loving Lettuce

Q: Why is lettuce the most loving vegetable?

A: Because it's all heart.

Party Hard

Q: Why is Valentine's Day a great day for a party?

A: Because you can party hearty.

My Better Half

Q: What did the toast say to the butter on Valentine's Day?

A: You're my butter half!

One in a Million

Q: What did one watermelon say to the other on Valentine's Day?

A: You're one in a melon!

Halloween

A Demon's Bff

Q: Why do demons and ghouls hang out together?

A: Because demons are a ghouls best friend!

- - - - - - - - - ★ ALEXA'S FAVORITE

Skeleton Weatherman

Q: How did the skeleton know it was going to rain on Halloween?

A: He could feel it in his bones!

- -

Interrupting Ghost

Q: What did the mummy ghost say to the noisy young ghost who kept interrupting?

A: "Spook when you're spooken to."

The Witch's Garage

Q: What do you call a witch's garage?

A: A broom closet.

Skeleton Chase

Q: Why did the skeleton climb up the tree?

A: Because a dog was after his bones!

Cemetery Story

Q: Why is a cemetery a great place to write a story?

A: Because there are so many plots there!

Dracula's Dog

Q: What dog breed would Dracula love to have as a pet?

A: Bloodhound!

Gargling Vampire

Q: Why did the vampire need mouthwash?

A: Because he had bat breath.

Sitting by the Fire

Q: What happened to the skeleton who stayed by the fire for too long?

A: He became bone dry.

Locked Cemetery

Q: How do you get inside a locked cemetery at night?

A: Use a Skeleton Key to unlock the gates!

I Don't Boo-Lieve You

Q: Why are ghosts bad liars?

A: Because you can see right through them.

Just Relax

Q: Why are skeletons so calm?

A: Because nothing gets under their skin!

- - - - - - - - - ★ **ALEXA'S FAVORITE**

Boo-tiful Hair

Q: What do ghosts use to wash their hair?

A: Sham-BOO!

- -

Lonely Skeletons

Q: Why don't skeletons ever go trick-or-treating?

A: Because they have no body to go with.

Sick Zombie

Q: Why didn't the zombie go to school?

A: He felt rotten!

Lovable Monsters

Q: What does the ghost call his true love?

A: My ghoul-friend.

Mummy Music

Q: What genre of music does a mummy like the best?

A: Wrap!

Perfect Recipe

Q: What does the skeleton chef say when he serves you a meal?

A: "Bone Appetit!"

Sated Vampire

Q: How can you tell when a vampire has been in a bakery?

A: All the jelly has been sucked out of the jelly doughnuts.

Dracula's Renovations

Q: What's it called when a vampire has trouble with his house?

A: A grave problem.

Ghosts on Vacation

Q: Where do ghosts like to travel on vacation?

A: The Dead Sea!

Signed, Sealed, Delivered

Q: How do vampires start their letters?

A: "Tomb it may concern…"

Squashed Squash

Q: How do you mend a broken Jack-o-lantern?

A: With a pumpkin patch.

At Least She Has a Good Sun Hat!

Q: What do you call a witch who lives on a beach?

A: A sand-witch.

Italian Ghosts

Q: What do Italian ghosts have for dinner?

A: Spook-hetti!

Busy Mummy

Q: Why don't mummies take time off?

A: They're afraid to unwind.

Vampire Fruit

Q: Which fruit is a vampire's favorite?

A: Neck-tarine!

Superstitious Rodent

Q: When is it bad luck to be followed by a black cat?

A: When you're a mouse.

Good-Humored Monster

Q: What goes Ha-ha-ha-ha!, thud!!! and keeps laughing?

A: A monster laughing its head off!

That Candy Is for the Birds

Q: What do birds say on Halloween to get candy?

A: Twick-or-tweet

Ghost Glasses

Q: What do ghosts wear when their eyesight gets blurred?

A: Spooktacles

Thanksgiving

Already Full

Q: Who is not hungry at Thanksgiving?

A: The turkey, because he's already stuffed!

Belt Buckle

Q: Why does a pilgrim's pants always fall down?

A: Because they wear their belt buckle on their hat.

Ill-Mannered Turkeys

Q: Why do turkeys always go, "gobble, gobble"?

A: Because they never learned good table manners!

Dancing on Thanksgiving

Q: What's the best dance to do on Thanksgiving?

A: The turkey trot.

Smelling Dinner

Q: What smells the best at a Thanksgiving dinner?

A: Your nose.

Drive-Through Thanksgiving

Q: What do you call a running turkey?

A: Fast food.

Fowl Play

Q: Why did the police arrest the turkey?

A: They suspected fowl play.

Small vs. Large

Q: If you call a large turkey a gobbler, what do you call a small one?

A: Goblet.

Math Pie

Q: What do you get if you divide the circumference of a pumpkin by its diameter?

A: Pumpkin pi.

Stuffed Turkey

Q: What's the best way to stuff a turkey?

A: Serve him lots of pizza and ice cream!

The Perfect Weather

Q: What kind of weather does a turkey like?

A: Fowl weather!

Don't Let the Turkey Near the Dessert

Q: Why should you never set the turkey next to the dessert?

A: Because he will gobble, gobble it up!

Thanksgiving Attire

Q: What do you wear to Thanksgiving dinner?

A: A Har-VEST.

Don't Mistake Me for a Chicken

Q: Why did the turkey cross the road twice?

A: To prove he wasn't a chicken!

Sporty Pumpkin

Q: What is a pumpkin's favorite sport?

A: Squash.

Turkey Fight

Q: What happened when the turkey got into a fight?

A: He got the stuffing knocked out of him!

Haunted Turkey

Q: What would you get if you crossed a turkey with a ghost?

A: A poultrygeist!

Musical Turkey

Q: What do you get when you cross a turkey with a harp?

A: A bird who can pluck itself.

If Your Father Could See You Now

Q: What did the mother turkey say to her disobedient children?

A: If your father could see you now, he'd turn over in his gravy.

Thanksgiving Flour

Q: What do you use to make Thanksgiving bread?

A: May flour.

---------- ★ **ALEXA'S FAVORITE**

Locked Out

Q: What key won't open any door?

A: A turkey!

Christmas

Celestial Greeting

Q: How do Christmas angels greet each other?

A: "Halo!"

Time Flies When You're Having Fun

Q: Why did Santa put a clock in his sleigh?

A: Because he wanted to see time fly!

Now We Know

Q: Why does Santa go down the chimney?

A: Because it soots him!

Singing Elf

Q: What do you call an elf who sings?

A: A wrapper!

114

---------- ★ **ALEXA'S FAVORITE**

No Umbrellas at the North Pole?

Q: Why are Comet, Cupid, Donner, and Blitzen always wet?

A: Because they are rain deer.

Christmas Cut

Q: Why did the Christmas tree go to the barber?

A: It needed to be trimmed.

Santa Goes Shopping

Q: Why did Santa bring 22 reindeer to Walmart?

A: Because what he wanted to buy cost around 20 bucks, but just in case it was more, he brought some extra doe.

Bad Grades for Rudolph

Q: Why didn't Rudolph get a good report card?

A: Because he went down in history.

Santa's in Debt

Q: What do you call a bankrupt Santa?

A: Saint Nickel-less.

---------- ★ ALEXA'S FAVORITE

Laughing All the Way!

Q: What is a lion's favorite Christmas carol?

A: Jungle Bells.

- -

Ho-Ho-Ow

Q: What's red and white and falls down chimneys?

A: Santa Klutz!

Scrooge's Favorite Pet

Q: Why did Scrooge keep a pet lamb?

A: Because it would say, "Baaaaahh humbug!"

Green Thumb

Q: Why does Santa have three garden plots up at the North Pole?

A: That way he can hoe, hoe, hoe!

Reindeer Spotting

Q: Where do you find reindeer?

A: It depends on where you leave them!

They Love It Deerly

Q: Why do Dasher and Dancer love coffee?

A: Because they're Santa's star bucks!

Scary Santa

Q: What do you call people who are afraid of Santa Claus?

A: Claustrophobic.

Up on the Housetop

Q: How much did Santa pay for his sleigh?

A: Nothing. It was on the house!

Great White Christmas

Q: Who delivers Christmas presents to good little sharks when they're sleeping?

A: Santa Jaws!

Santa Speak

Q: What is Santa's primary language?

A: North Polish.

Berry Ambitious

Q: Where do Christmas plants go when they want to become movie stars?

A: Holly-wood!

---------- ★ **ALEXA'S FAVORITE**

Oh Deer

Q: Which of Santa's reindeer has the worst manners?

A: RUDE-olph, of course!

Don't Forget the Bow and Arrow

Q: What do you call an outlaw who steals gift-wrapping from the rich to give to the poor?

A: Ribbon Hood.

---------- ★ **ALEXA'S FAVORITE**

Santa the Martial Artist

Q: How do you know Santa Claus is good at karate?

A: He has a black belt!

His Favorite Is the Double (Christmas) Tree

Q: Where does Santa stay when he's on vacation?

A: At a ho-ho-ho-tel.

Holiday Half Bath

Q: How does Santa keep his bathroom tiles immaculate?

A: He uses Comet.

Scrooge Touchdown

Q: How did Scrooge win the football game?

A: The ghost of Christmas passed.

Good Luck Getting Grumpy to Make Toys

Q: Why does Santa have elves in his workshop?

A: Because the Seven Dwarfs were busy!

Christmas Trees

Q: Why are Christmas trees such bad knitters?

A: They are always dropping their needles.

Ho-Ho-Oh!

Q: Who says, Oh, oh, oh?

A: Santa Claus walking backward.

Last Laughs

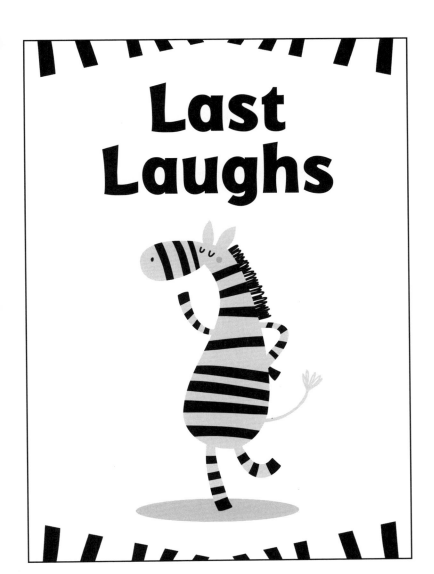

Don't Brake My Bike!

The first time my little brother was on a bike with training wheels, I shouted, "Step back on the pedals, and the bike will brake!"

He nodded and still rode straight into the bush.

"Why didn't you push back on the pedals?" I asked, helping him up.

"You said if I did, the bike would break."

Axe-ing for the Truth

Teacher: "George Washington not only chopped down his father's cherry tree but also admitted it.

Now, Joey, do you know why his father didn't punish him?"

Joey: "Because George still had the axe in his hand?"

Rabbit Food

An adorable little girl walked into my pet shop and asked, "Excuse me, do you have any rabbits here?"

"I do," I answered, and leaning down to her eye level, I asked, "Did you want a white rabbit or would you rather have a soft, fuzzy black rabbit?"

She shrugged. "I don't think my python really cares."

Soup-er Bug

A boy asks his father, "Dad, are bugs good to eat?"

"That's disgusting. Don't talk about things like that over dinner," the dad replies.

After dinner the father asks, "Now, son, what did you want to ask me?"

"Oh, nothing," the boy says. "There was a bug in your soup, but now it's gone."

Beary Close

What does it mean when you find a bear with a wet nose?

It means you're too close to the bear.

Rapid Robbery

A turtle is crossing the road when he's mugged by two snails. When the police show up, they ask him what happened. The shaken turtle replies, "I don't know. It all happened so fast."

Dangerous Crossing

Two hedgehogs on the side of a road wanted to cross the street. As they approached the crosswalk, one says, "Don't cross here!" The other one says, "Why not?"

The first one says, "Look what happened to the zebra!"

Schooling Mom

My older son loves school, but his younger brother absolutely hates it. One weekend he cried and fretted and tried every excuse not to go back on Monday. Sunday morning on the way home from church, the crying and whining built to a crescendo. At the end of my rope, I finally stopped the car and explained, "Honey, it's a law. If you don't go to school, they'll put Mommy in jail."

He looked at me, thought a moment, then asked, "How long would you have to stay?"

Black and White

A pair of cows were talking in the field. One says, "Have you heard about the mad cow disease that's around?"

"Yes," the other cow says. "Makes me glad I'm a penguin."

Name-Calling

My five-year-old nephew has always happily answered to BJ. That ended when he came home from his first day of school in a foul mood. It seems his teacher took roll, and he never heard his name.

"Why didn't anyone tell me my name was William?" he complained.

Lost Child

Concerned when one of his most reliable workers doesn't show up, the boss calls the employee's home. The phone is answered by a giggling child.

"Is your dad home?" the boss asks.

"Yes."

"May I speak to him?"

"No."

"Well, can I speak with your mom?"

"No. She's with the policeman."

Alarmed, the boss says, "Gosh. Well then, may I speak with the policeman?"

"No. He's busy talking to the man in the helicopter that's bringing in the search team."

"My goodness!" says the boss, now really worried. "What are they searching for?"

"Me," the kid chortles.

Forceful Gifts

Suddenly in the middle of the fight, Darth Vader pulls Luke to him and whispers, "I know what you're getting for Christmas!"

Luke exclaims, "But how??!?"

"It's true, Luke." (Breathes) "I know what you're getting for Christmas."

Luke tries to ignore this. He tears himself free, screaming, "How could you know this?!"

Vader replies, "I felt your presents."

Also Available from Reader's Digest

Laughter, the Best Medicine

Drawn from one of the most popular features of *Reader's Digest* magazine, this lighthearted collection of jokes, one-liners, and other glimpses of life is just what the doctor ordered.

ISBN 978-0-89577-977-9 • $9.95 paperback

Laughter Really Is the Best Medicine

Guaranteed to put laughter in your day, this side-splitting compilation of jokes pokes fun at the facts and foibles of daily routines. This little volume is sure to tickle your funny bone.

ISBN 978-1-60652-204-2 • $9.95 paperback

Laughter Still Is the Best Medicine

This hilarious collection offers up some of the funniest moments that get us through our day, with jokes, gags, and cartoons that will have readers laughing out loud.

ISBN 978-1-62145-137-2 • $9.99 paperback

Laughter Totally Is the Best Medicine

More than 1,000 of the funniest, laugh-out-loud jokes, quips, quotes, anecdotes, and cartoons from *Reader's Digest* magazine—guaranteed to put laughter in your day.

ISBN 978-1-62145-406-9 • $9.99 paperback

For more information, visit us at RDTradePublishing.com
E-book editions are also available.

Reader's Digest books can be purchased through retail and online bookstores.